STOP RESISTING

The Law Enforcement Officer's Guide to Proven Control Tactics, Less Lawsuits, and Building Community Trust Through Martial Arts

Jeremy Butler, Ph.D.

Published by Pagoda Rebirth Press.

For more information, email
policetraining@jeremybutlerphd.com.

Cover design and formatting by MiblArt.
Edited by Janet Toliver, Psy.D.
ISBN: 979-8-9863642-0-9 (paperback)
ISBN: 979-8-9863642-1-6 (ebook)

This book is dedicated to early career police officers, who are the future and source for change in the law enforcement field.

Contents

Introduction

First of all, thank you. Thank you for investing your time and money to educate yourself on the critical topic of improving police use of force performance through martial arts training. This book was written with two groups of individuals in mind: police officers and martial arts instructors. Connecting these two entities nationwide will help law enforcement obtain the training they need to do their jobs safely and effectively. Whether you are an officer, instructor or even a concerned civilian, you are needed. In this book, you will learn everything you need to know to take a proactive role in getting the best training possible for law enforcement. Use of force training is largely underfunded and undervalued in the police community, and the martial arts community holds a solution to this problem. Martial arts can offer a unique, controlled environment for officers to practice safe and effective techniques, leading to less injuries and safer arrests. This book will cover the most applicable techniques for law enforcement and how to find the right martial arts academy that suits the needs of a police officer.

Let me first say that physical training is just one of several areas needed to improve officer safety, civilian safety, and police-community relations. Other areas include more minority representation in law enforcement, addressing implicit racial bias, changes in policy, among others. This book does not aim to ignore these critical issues; it is simply not the aim of this particular text. I'm writing this book based on over 20 years of martial arts training, 7 years of law enforcement experience, and an expertise in police non-lethal force training.

During this time, I noticed many issues from both communities (police and martial arts) that if appropriately addressed, would create an excellent solution to the police use of force training problem. I've seen martial arts instructors with no law enforcement background offer poor advice to police officers on control tactics. I've also seen poorly trained police officers struggle with subduing subjects resulting in various outcomes including severe injuries to the officer and excessive force incidents on the part of the officer. Neither the instructor nor the officer in these situations should be completely scorned. I have no doubt that martial arts instructors have much to offer the law enforcement community and those who have police officers as students offer them information that they truly believe to be of value for the officers. I also believe the vast majority of officers have zero interest in getting into unnecessary physical encounters let alone intentionally using excessive force. But there are a number of standard skills and tactics that instructors should implement into their training to ensure they position their officers for success. Additionally, officers working in departments with little to no consistent training in control tactics deserve to know how to find the right martial art for them as well as the best training methods and techniques for law enforcement. This book will bridge that gap between the police community and the martial arts community to educate officers with critical control tactics training tips and will better prepare instructors for teaching their art to them.

1

The Use of Force Training Problem

Police use of force practices is a controversial area in the U.S. Countless excessive force complaints and lawsuits, juxtaposed with physical assaults on officers every year, paint a clear picture that police-community relations are pretty tense and need improvement. Considering this issue is tremendously multifaceted, it also needs a multifaceted solution that will reduce incidents of excessive force, improve officer safety, and enhance relationships between police and the community. The one critical component that connects all these issues is TRAINING.

Officers are simply not given enough training for handling non-lethal use of force encounters, specifically in circumstances where deadly force is not warranted. However, since use of force is fluid and situations can quickly escalate to deadly force in an instant, any commentary on deadly force will be from that context. Why focus on non-lethal force? Because it allows officers to train for situations that they are significantly more likely to encounter. According to the FBI (as cited by U.S. Dept of Justice, 2021), between 2011 and 2020, 553,506 officers were physically assaulted in the United States. In 2020, approximately 74% of the 60,105 attacks on officers were carried out using personal bodily weapons, such as fists, feet, and takedowns. Officers sustained injuries approximately 26% of the time (U.S. Dept of Justice, 2021). Also, some estimate that officers use force in only 1.4% of the millions of contacts in the U.S. each year, and in most cases, the force is low level (Hough, 2017). Overall, officers are significantly more likely to use non-lethal force on duty than lethal force.

Many of the use of force incidents that turn deadly often start out non-lethal, then escalate to actions that result in the use of deadly force, whether accidental or intentional. The high-profile cases in recent years, such as Eric Garner, Walter Scott, Rayshard Brooks, and Jonathan Price, are examples of circumstances where the end result was impacted by the officers' subject control and tactical decision-making performance when faced with non-compliance. Yes, there are situations where deadly force is the most reasonable choice. For example, if a subject has a deadly weapon and they are actively using it, or showing intent to use it, responding with deadly force is certainly reasonable. But these clear-cut cases are neither the problem nor the norm.

The reality is, throughout an officer's career, they are more likely to encounter non-lethal force incidents that could escalate to death or serious injury without proper training. The level of training an officer receives beyond the academy depends largely on the department standards, budgets, and personal experiences.

> **"Expect the best. Prepare for the worst. Capitalize on what comes."**
>
> — Zig Ziglar

In the U.S., police training is entirely decentralized. States vary in their standards in pre-service training (i.e., police academy) and annual in-service training requirements. In fact, before the 1960s, police training in America was unstructured and largely informal (Alpert & Dunham, 1997; Walker, 1999). The law enforcement industry has since improved and formalized its training standards, but the variability in requirements and resources across agencies remains the same. Additionally, with nearly 18,000 law enforcement agencies in the U.S., the vast majority (approximately 75%) have fewer than 25 officers (International Association of Chiefs of Police, 2018; Roberg et al., 2009). These circumstances come with fewer resources for departmental de-escalation and use of force training. This can result in resistance from administration to offer consistent control tactics training due to concerns such as fear of officer injury and limited staffing. Officers in larger departments with adequate resources for training also face barriers, such as general disinterest from officers and administration and lack of appreciation for its value. Among others, these barriers seem to supersede the pursuit of quality training across all departments.

This lack of training comes with consequences for many officers, not only in use of force but also as it relates to physical fitness for duty. I once responded to a medical call for a person found unconscious on the 7th floor of a college residence hall. When I arrived at the building, the elevator was unavailable, and I knew waiting for it could possibly mean the difference between life and death for the subject. I sprinted up the stairs as quickly as I could, and by the time I made it to the 4th floor, my legs (and lungs) were giving out due to fatigue. I continued to push myself to make it up the stairs while sweating profusely and gasping for air. When I arrived at the 7th floor and connected with the subject, I was so out of breath I could barely speak. It took me way longer to get there than it should have. Luckily, the person was okay and was cleared by the paramedics soon after, but this incident left a substantial impact on me. Imagine if the subject had died because I didn't make it there in time to help due to my poor physical conditioning. Imagine if there was a use of force encounter when I arrived and I could barely keep myself standing, let alone handle a resisting subject in that moment. Imagine if it was an officer down and I was supposed to be the backup unit. Processing all of these possibilities gave me a boost of motivation to take my cardiovascular and anaerobic endurance training more seriously. I thought I was in pretty good shape. Still, that incident was a rude awakening that my fitness level was substandard, especially when considering the addition of body armor and a 20-plus pound duty belt around my waist.

Performing tasks like the ones described above won't turn out well for the officer who becomes complacent in their physical conditioning. Not to mention, studies have found correlations between physical fitness and use of force tasks such as controlling and arresting subjects (Arvey et al., 1992; Dillern et al., 2014; Wilmore & Davis, 1979). While there seems to be more support and value placed on consistent fitness training in the law enforcement community, there is still work to be done in this area. Police officers are more likely to be obese, have high blood pressure, and have an increased risk for heart attacks than the average person (International Association of Chiefs of Police, 2018). Although officers often enter the field in optimal shape due to the police academy training, their fitness levels decline as they age due to being less active and succumbing to the sedentary nature of the job. This is a problem that we as a society must address both for the safety of the officers as well as the public. The solution starts with a realization that many departments don't have (or aren't willing to provide) the training resources officers need for long term success. Therefore, the responsibility for training and overall wellness must fall on officers as it is their lives on the line. When this is accepted, officers can take matters into their own hands and leverage one another as well as the support of the community to get the training they need.

Ironically, the dual benefit of martial arts training on fitness and control tactics make it the perfect option for addressing both of these concerns. I am the first to admit that if it weren't for martial arts, I wouldn't be anywhere near as active as I am. Martial arts training is a challenging, progressive, physically and mentally stimulating activity that works the entire body. Try putting five minutes on a clock and attempt to gain complete control over a live resisting 150-pound Brazilian jiu-jitsu brown belt without becoming gassed and forced to submit several times. You will quickly notice the dual benefit of this type of training on physical conditioning and its direct applicability to a force encounter.

Some officers are hesitant to train due to a fear of injury. While this is a legitimate concern, we must consider the ratio of risk versus reward. Yes, an officer could possibly get injured while training and require paid time off during recovery. However, the nature of police work is risky, and a training injury is much less likely to be as severe as an injury sustained during a real encounter with an officer that lacks consistent training. Picture these two scenarios.

Scenario 1: In a midsize department, the majority of officers actively train in some form of control tactics or martial arts at least once a week. Every year, maybe 5 officers sustain minor injuries that require them to take a few days off work. Due to the consistency and realism behind their training, officers are more confident and skilled in handling situations. This resulted in a significantly lower number of departmental use of force encounters and excessive force complaints.

Scenario 2: In this department, officers receive their standard annual use of force training. These trainings generally run smoothly and officers simply review the curriculum they've used for many years. Injuries happen but not often and they usually involve minor complaints from officers with pre-existing injuries. Officers in this department have a relatively high number of use of force incidents every year where approximately 5 to 10 officers sustain injuries but excessive force complaints are high and continuing to increase. The department also has one officer who was recently hospitalized after an encounter with an intoxicated high school football player and one pending multimillion-dollar excessive force lawsuit against several officers.

Neither of these scenarios are ideal, but the first one is ultimately best for the overall health of a department and its officers. Consistent realistic training breeds skilled officers who are more likely to maintain physical and emotional control. They are also less likely to overreact during use of force encounters. This will ultimately save departments more money long-term while also keeping their officers safe. Policing is a profession where we often accept the risks associated with handling dangerous calls for service but are unwilling to accept the risks associated with effective training to prepare for these situations.

Training outside one's agency (e.g., martial arts) could also be concerning because officers may use techniques that are against department policy, which could lead to disciplinary action or lawsuits. Again, a legitimate concern but let's look at it from a different perspective. Being trained affords officers with the ability to think more clearly and make better decisions under stress in comparison to those who only fulfill the minimum standards. In some areas, these department standards for control tactics training can be as minute as a 2-day course every 2 to 3 years. Martial arts are not just about learning techniques to use on the job, it is about the psychological transformation that occurs from training consistently. Departments can still enforce policies for use of force and require that officers training martial arts outside the agency follow them. For those concerned about this, the agency can build professional relationships with the martial arts schools in their area in order to recommend the martial arts training programs most consistent with their use of force policies.

From the officer's perspective, a general concern with martial arts training is the time commitment. The odd work hours required of an officer, especially an early career officer, makes time a major commodity. Committing hours away from home for training, oftentimes on days off, can be a lot to ask of an officer and their family. Understanding that this sacrifice is necessary to help ensure they make it home to their family every night may help put things into perspective. This kind of training is more than just a hobby for a law enforcement officer, it's a necessity. The next chapter will outline more specifically how the police community can leverage the martial arts community for training, along with examples of success in this area.

Martial Arts as a Solution

Martial arts training is rooted in self-preservation by way of various strategies depending on the civilization and culture. These strategies may include striking with different parts of the body, wrestling, ground grappling, joint locks, use of weaponry, or a combination of these. Many agencies may dismiss the idea of their officers becoming martial artists but the reality is that police arrest and control tactics are derived from various styles of martial arts. The techniques are just adapted to meet a law enforcement objective, which is to apply the minimum force necessary to gain control of a subject. With that, there is a clear opportunity to gain direct access to consistent training in the methods that serve as the source for these techniques via the martial arts community.

In the U.S., the number of martial arts studios are estimated at over 45,000 (IBISWorld, 2021).

The bottom line is there are many options for police communities to explore to develop partnerships with, so officers have an opportunity to train. This professional partnership can manifest in many different ways. The martial arts academy could host workshops on police defensive tactics, develop law enforcement only classes, or officers could attend regular classes. The former two options are perfect for officers who aren't willing to commit the time to train multiple days per week, are hesitant to begin their journey among civilians, or are not interested in learning a complete martial art but have interest in techniques directly applicable to law enforcement. Not only do these options create a win-win situation for the martial arts business and the police officers, but it also strengthens community relations and team cohesion among officers. What better way to build relationships in your community and with fellow officers than to struggle, develop a skill, and make progress on the mats together?

Agencies all over the country consistently hold community policing events to create opportunities for civilians to get to know officers in their area (Maryland Community Policing Institute, n.d.). Common examples include short term, 1-day programs like "Coffee with a Cop," "Shop with a Cop," and "Ride-A-Longs." Additionally, longer term initiatives include school resource officer programs, youth and citizen police academies, and the Special Olympics philanthropy. Martial arts training is an additional long-term solution for building community trust.

An officer who trains regularly at a local martial arts academy will develop relationships with people from all walks of life, build a skillset that could possibly save their lives, and potentially change negative perceptions some may have about police.

I've been on many martial arts training mats with good people who have made mistakes in the past and had negative run-ins with law enforcement. While these experiences left many of them with a distrust of law enforcement, brief conversations have cleared up so many misconceptions that drove their anger. Even those who persisted in their negative perspectives, often insisted that I was "just one of the few good ones." This is a commonly held viewpoint when a civilian gets to know an officer outside of their official capacity. Ironically, the same officer may be viewed as one of the "bad ones" by others as soon as they put on the uniform. The point is that these negative perceptions are often more related to a lack of personal connection with those in law enforcement than officer misconduct. Martial arts academies offer a neutral ground for officers and civilians to get more positive interactions with one another. Below are several examples of how agencies can leverage the martial arts community for consistent, quality police training while building community relations.

In 2019, the Marietta Police Department in Marietta, Georgia partnered with a local Brazilian jiu-jitsu academy and required police recruits to attend at least one training session per week prior to beginning their field training officer (FTO) process (BJJ Training

Data, 2021). The success of the program led them to extend the training to all in-service officers, who were allowed to earn compensation time and POST (Peace Officer's Standards and Training) credit by attending classes up to three times a week. The goal was to provide officers with consistent defensive tactics training to build skill and confidence via an art that did not rely on striking techniques to gain compliance. The results of the initiative accomplished this goal plus so much more, including a 23% reduction in Taser deployments, 48% reduction in injuries to officers during force encounters, and a 53% reduction in serious injuries to suspects during force encounters. It should be noted that the data was not collected under the standards of a well-controlled research study, which may impact the reliability of the results. Regardless, this example demonstrates the value of both developing partnerships with the martial arts community and its potential impact on use of force performance. Since this initiative, multiple agencies have followed suit by pursuing similar partnerships with local martial arts academies. However, as previously discussed, not all agencies will have the funding or willingness to pay for this type of training. Regardless of whether or not an agency supports these initiatives, there are alternative options and officers must take responsibility for their training.

The "Adopt-a-Cop" Brazilian Jiu-Jitsu (BJJ) program is an excellent model for bridging the gap between the police and martial arts community. This non-profit program allows active-duty patrol officers to train at any affiliated BJJ academy tuition free until they earn the rank of blue belt. Most individuals who obtain a blue belt in BJJ are equipped with the ability to control a larger inexperienced person on the ground. This skill is paramount during an arrest of a resisting suspect. Even if an officer chooses to train at a BJJ academy that is not affiliated with Adopt-a-Cop BJJ, the organization will still pay a portion of the officer's monthly tuition to help offset the cost. This program is a critical solution for addressing the financial barrier of consistent training and creating change in the law enforcement community. If you are a police officer, martial arts instructor, or civilian interested in getting involved, you can find more information at www.adoptacopbjj.org.

USA Judo has taken a unique approach to this initiative by establishing a program involving both police training and youth development work (Bleiker, 2021). The USA Judo P3 Program model facilitates workshops in judo-based arrest and control techniques; provides agencies with assistance in developing youth judo programs where officers can teach and mentor youth to build positive police-community interactions; and builds judo-based law enforcement initiatives for colleges with law-enforcement related degree programs. This is another prime example of how martial arts can also be used as a vehicle to improve police-community relations. The techniques taught in the program were developed by police officers with the needs of patrol and SWAT officers in mind. Several high-level judo practitioners, who are also police officers, serve as task force members for the training offering the curriculum in a "train the trainer" structure. This format, which is quite popular in the law enforcement industry, involves officers being taught the techniques and training methods, then return to their departments with a certification to train their colleagues. The program also offers free memberships to USA Judo for officers who participate in the trainings. If you are interested in more information on the USA Judo P3 Program, you can visit www.teamusa.org/ USA-Judo.

While the USA Judo P3 Program is a great initiative that is highly recommended, the "train the trainer" structure in the law enforcement training domain has many strengths and limitations. It offers great benefits to agencies with budgetary constraints because they won't have to pay course registration fees for every officer in the department. When an officer has genuine interest in instructing, it can transform the training culture of the department. Officers can have multiple formal and informal in-service trainings throughout the year to aid in long-term skill retention.

While there are numerous great control tactics programs that include this model, the amount of time it often takes to be considered a "certified instructor" can be problematic. Many of these training structures involve only 40 hours of instruction in the curriculum and teaching methods before participants are certified. This short timeline (typically in a 1-week format) makes it difficult for anyone to learn to teach a skillset as complex as control tactics, especially with no previous experience. Although it is a popular training structure in law enforcement, the "train the trainer" programs do not allow for an expert level knowledge of the material. Instructors may come out of the trainings with a lack of depth in understanding the techniques and either a lack of confidence in their ability to deliver the content, or a belief that they know more than they do.

> **"Teaching is the highest form of understanding."**
>
> — Aristotle

To maximize the effectiveness of the "train the trainer" model, agencies can and should create a consistent training schedule. New instructors in these courses have a small window of time immediately following the course before they begin to lose details in how to perform the techniques. They also need to complete thousands more repetitions themselves before they truly understand the techniques. With that, the best follow-up step for agencies that use this model is to get their new instructors teaching the skills immediately upon returning to the department. The more time that passes before the trainer can teach (and practice) the material, the less likely they will remember the correct execution of the techniques. Some programs, such as Gracie Survival Tactics

(GST), offer supplemental materials in the form of online technical breakdowns for instructors. This is an excellent resource to help refresh instructors on the techniques to teach them accurately and effectively.

Regardless, the process of getting instructors teaching quickly doesn't have to be formal. Implementing open training days can allow officers to sign up and train for a couple hours before or after shift. If departments are not equipped with the space to offer departmental control tactics training, this could be a perfect opportunity to reach out to larger departments nearby, or even local martial arts academies to use the space. It's about using your resources and problem solving.

Retired Lieutenant, Dr. Michael Schlosser, who worked for Rantoul Police Department in Illinois, utilized his martial arts academy as a site for extra training. On nights with minimal calls for service, he would often have officers meet at his academy for training. This gave him and his officers the opportunity to get consistent repetition of the skills at no additional cost to the department. These trainings led to a weekly police control tactics class where officers shared their knowledge from various backgrounds including striking arts, grappling arts, and team arrest and control tactics. Contrary to commonly held beliefs that this presents high injury risks, the positive training environment allowed for these trainings to go on for many years without any major injuries.

City Channel 4 (2017) covered a news story on the Iowa City Police Department and University of Iowa Police accomplishing their training goals by partnering with the University of Iowa Wrestling Team. Officers worked with the wrestling coaches and athletes on effective subject control, takedowns, and takedown defense on the university campus. The ultimate goal of collegiate wrestling is to take your opponent to the ground and pin them. These techniques have a significant applicability to the needs of a police officer. Collaboration between police and athletic departments build both positive relationships with the community and gives officers practical training for use of force. University police departments are especially encouraged to seek similar training opportunities and collaborations in their campus community.

The examples given above illustrate unique ways that the police community can leverage the martial arts community for training. However, sometimes officers must seek this training on their own. While finding consistent training can be challenging, it is well worth the effort and commitment. If you value it, you will find creative solutions to make it happen. If you don't, you will make excuses for why it can't happen.

Perhaps the greatest benefit of regular martial arts training is it enhances motor learning, or what many refer to as "muscle memory." Motor learning is the relatively permanent improvement in a motor skill due to practice or experience (Haywood & Getchell, 2020). Just as with any skill, consistent martial arts practice can strengthen the neural pathways in the brain to enhance your performance of these movement patterns. Fitts and Posner's (1967) Stages of Motor Learning explains the process of motor skill acquisition in simple terms. This well-known theory proposes that learning a motor skill (e.g., executing a basic throw) occurs in three stages: cognitive, associative, and autonomous stage (Fitts & Posner, 1967). These stages can be used to understand the process of mastering skills such as the techniques in a martial arts or control tactics curriculum.

The cognitive stage involves consciously processing the skill (Fitts & Posner, 1967). Learners with little or no experience exhibit considerable cognitive effort to execute the movement. In this stage, errors tend to be numerous and learners are dependent on instructor feedback to improve. With practice, learners experience quick gains in skill. For example, one of the first throws learned in judo is osoto gari (major outer reap). This throw involves multiple movements including an off-balance using grips on the opponent's lapel and sleeve, a step with one leg, and a big reaping motion with the other leg to the back of the opponent's calf, taking them to the ground. A learner in the cognitive stage may frequently take a step with the wrong leg, forget to off-balance their partner first, and require repeated technical corrections by the instructor during this stage.

At the associative stage, the learner now understands the basic components of the movement and can begin to refine specific details that enhance performance of the skill (Fitts & Posner, 1967). While they still make mistakes, they are less frequent than in the cognitive stage. After a couple weeks of practicing the osoto gari throw, the learner can now execute the technique without being given instructions and start catching their own mistakes and correcting them. This stage tends to last longer than the cognitive stage.

The final stage, autonomous stage, can take years to reach and many never reach it. In the autonomous stage, the skill can be performed with little to no conscious thought (Fitts & Posner, 1967). After years of practice and thousands of repetitions, the learner can execute the osoto gari throw against a training partner or opponent under live resistance the moment they feel the opening. They've become so comfortable with the movement they can focus on other things like avoiding the opponent's attacks and other potential threats in the environment. Consistent martial arts training over time can bring officers into the autonomous stage in performing techniques that they may need to save their lives. This level of skill will be difficult to attain if relying on infrequent departmental control tactics in-service trainings.

The problem with many training curricula, including in law enforcement agencies and martial arts schools, is the lack of willingness to practice under live resistance and pressure test the techniques once they've passed the cognitive stage. This is absolutely critical, especially for law enforcement who must often rely on these techniques for their own survival. Since learning the techniques take commitment and years of practice, understanding what arts would be most suited to the needs of the job is paramount. The details on the martial arts best known for embracing the pressure testing philosophy, along with what officers should look for in a martial arts academy, will be discussed at length in the chapters to follow.

The Best Martial Arts for Law Enforcement (and Why)

There is no national standard for police control tactics. Some agencies use a force continuum where the officer must use techniques that are proportionate to the level of force they are faced with in the situation. Some agencies have a control tactics curriculum that officers must adhere to in an encounter with little autonomy in technique selection. Other agency standards are broader in nature and focus only on whether the officer's actions were in line with established use of force case law (e.g., Tennessee v Garner and Graham v Connor). Regardless of the agency's use of force policy, officers who want consistent control tactics training often have to seek it outside of their agency. So, in this chapter we'll discuss the best martial arts for law enforcement.

> **"It is not the style, but the man behind the style that makes it work."**
>
> — James A. Jones, Jr.

Nearly every martial art has something to offer to law enforcement. When the training is provided in a practical way, the specific style becomes less important. As long as there is a healthy combination of reality-based training, regular sparring, and technical proficiency training, it becomes a matter of personal preference. For the purposes of this book, martial arts training will be categorized into 3 areas: striking, weapons, and grappling. Below, each category will be explained in more detail.

Striking Arts

Striking-based martial arts focus on the execution of techniques such as punches, kicks, elbow strikes, and knee strikes while standing. Examples include karate, tae kwon do, boxing, kenpo, and Muay Thai. Some striking arts focus on one group of techniques, while others include a variety of striking methods. For example, boxers are restricted to using punches, while arts like karate and Muay Thai include all of the techniques listed above. But focusing on a small group of techniques is not necessarily a negative thing. Many people will argue that boxing offers the best option in developing the ability to punch and defend against punches in a fight. This is a direct result of decades of focus on that particular range. The same argument can be made for kicks in tae kwon do. While this Korean art involves more than just kicking, its focus on this area has made it the primary art many people think of if their aim is to develop kicking ability.

> "Everyone has a plan until they get punched in the mouth."
>
> — Mike Tyson

Understanding the striking range is important in law enforcement because it is often the default option when a violent attack is initiated. The last thing you want is to be attacked by a suspect without having trained in defending a barrage of punches. One solid strike to the face can completely take the fight out of anyone, especially if they've never experienced it. The more experience you have with strikes being thrown at you, even in a controlled training environment, the more comfortable you will be in handling them on the street.

Many police officers consider Muay Thai to be among the best martial arts for law enforcement (Butler, 2022). This striking-based art is known for its devastating leg kicks as well as knees, elbows, and sweeps from the clinch position. This style can prepare officers physically and mentally for the potential violence associated with real confrontations. The conditioning, drills, and sparring associated with the training can improve an officer's speed, power, cardiovascular endurance, and resilience. However, the violent nature of striking is not always suited for law enforcement. Even when justified, striking a suspect just looks bad. It can often result in a bloody face and black eyes for the suspect, and a fractured hand for the officer. The encounter will likely be recorded and, even if the officer acted within reason, the incident may result in a lawsuit and negative publicity for the department.

However, sometimes the officer must do what it takes to survive regardless to how it looks. That being said, training in striking is best used as a distraction tool for gaining control and for learning to defend against them. These elements make some exposure to striking arts critical for law enforcement. The development of defensive skill can be via using hands and forearms for blocking, using head movement or footwork for evasion, or closing the distance to clinch with the suspect. Regardless, striking arts allow police officers to build this comfort in dealing with strikes, especially punches. Adaptations should also be made to account for other variables unique to officers, such as weapons possessed by the officer and possibly the suspect during the arrests.

Weapon Arts

The second category of martial arts is weapon-based systems, which involve the use of weapons from various martial cultures. This includes arts like kendo, kobudo, krabi krabong, and kali. Considering weapons are so prevalent in American society, officers should understand their use and tactics for defending against them. However, most of the traditional weapon systems have limited applicability to the modern situations officers are likely to encounter. However, the Filipino martial arts of kali/arnis/escrima includes a variety of weapons, most commonly sticks and knives. Kali's unique philosophy is that any item can be used as a weapon, including pens, water bottles, umbrellas, newspapers, shoes, cell phones…literally anything. Practitioners often train using rattan sticks and are taught how the movements can apply to basically any item as well as in weaponless combat. Kali training can be a useful tool for law enforcement in two ways:

1. It can help maintain the officer's safety mindset that there are weapons everywhere and anything can be used as a weapon. Not to mention, every encounter involves a weapon because officers walk around with several around their waist. This often includes a baton, which is nearly identical in makeup to a kali stick.

2. During my time in law enforcement, there is no weapon that I came across more in my contacts with the public than pocket knives. Considering the knife training in kali is among the most developed in all martial arts, it is worth investing time in training with a qualified reality-based instructor. This will hopefully help reduce the urge to draw a firearm at close range against a knife without sufficient distance or control.

Caution must be taken, however, to distinguish between knife defense drills and training for the reality of a knife attack. A large foundation of the Filipino martial arts involves line familiarization through repetitive flow drills. While these are often criticized as impractical, they do have their place in learning the basic lines of attack and developing sensitivity in redirecting your training partner's energy. The problem is when practitioners fail to move beyond these drills and into training against unchoreographed violent attacks. There is no substitute to experiencing this kind of raw energy and realizing that simply drawing a gun against knife at close range is in most cases an unrealistic expectation. An officer needs practical solutions to dealing with weapons when there is no time to draw a weapon of their own. However, considering most use of force encounters are non-lethal and require sufficient subject control to effect the arrest, the number one category recommended for police would be a grappling art.

Grappling Arts

Grappling-based systems employ the philosophy of controlling the body at close range as opposed to using strikes to subdue a suspect. This can be achieved by applying some form of takedown (e.g., throws and sweeps) and/or joint manipulation in an effort to completely immobilize the individual. Examples of grappling-based styles include wrestling, judo, aikido, sambo, and Brazilian jiu-jitsu. Some arts, like aikido, tend to focus more on small joint manipulations and technical proficiency, while others such as judo, place more emphasis on the competitive spirit of attempting to throw, then control or submit an actively resisting opponent.

The grappling arts are ideal for law enforcement because their objective of close-range control and immobilization directly correlate with a police officers' goal in effecting an arrest. In fact, it is literally impossible to place an actively resisting subject in handcuffs without some form of grappling. The very action of putting the handcuffs on requires control of the upper extremities. With this, the top three grappling arts for law enforcement are wrestling, judo, and Brazilian jiu-jitsu due to their shared emphasis on training to control an individual under active resistance. This perspective is shared by many officers in the grappling community (Butler, 2022).

Four major forms of wrestling include folk-style, freestyle, Greco-Roman, and catch-as-catch-can. Although the way each of these combat sports are taught will be dependent on the instructor, there are characteristics that are consistent within each form based on the rules. While technique is definitely present in each of these forms of wrestling, strength is often emphasized. In general, you can expect an aggressive approach to accomplish the goal of getting the opponent to the ground and pinning them. Folk-style (collegiate) and freestyle (Olympic) wrestling both involve takedowns that allow you to attack the upper and lower body. Greco-Roman wrestling, on the other hand, does not allow practitioners to use their legs or attack their opponent's legs to execute a takedown. Although it may sound limiting, similar to what was discussed earlier, this reliance on upper body techniques arguably makes these athletes the best in the clinch. Catch-as-catch-can wrestling is the parent art of folk-style and freestyle. This style differs from the other forms in that it includes many submission holds in addition to the takedowns and pins.

Many officers may already have wrestling experience from high school, which could increase their willingness and interest in getting back into training. This experience may also benefit them greatly in subduing an actively resisting or fleeing suspect. For example, after being taken to the ground, resisting suspects often get back to their hands and knees, stand up, and attempt to get away. Fortunately, in wrestling there are entire systems of attack referred to as "breakdowns" and "mat returns," which were designed to address these types of situations. While the objectives are not the same, the techniques retain their effectiveness. Considering many opportunities for continued wrestling training beyond high school can be limited, those interested in pursuing the sport as a control tactics training tool should look into MMA gyms as many of them offer wrestling classes.

While the common wrestling approach of combining aggression with strength and technique is not a problem, it may be limiting to those who have a smaller frame or are naturally less aggressive. Judo, which is the parent art of Brazilian jiu-jitsu, was developed based on principles that address this issue. Judo translates to "gentle way" and was developed with the approach of applying maximal efficiency with minimal effort (Kano, 1986). Similar to catch wrestling, the aim of the sport is to take the opponent down, control, and/or submit them. The major difference is the greater emphasis on minimizing the amount of effort required to throw the opponent by using their energy and aggression to aid you in the technique. Judo is practiced using a gi, which is the uniform that can be used to execute the techniques. This factor may make judo slightly more appealing to smaller individuals than wrestling.

I remember my first experience grappling with a judo instructor, retired police officer, and mentor of mine from Chicago. It's easy to remember because

I ended up flat on my back within 20 seconds of him gripping my gi. The most mind-boggling part of the experience was how effortless and controlled it was. The round started with me attempting to off-balance him by pushing and pulling on this lapel. He calmly responded by moving with the force of the pushes and pulls. After that exchange, he slightly pulled on my lapel and as I tried to step forward to regain my balance, he swept my foot out from under me just before it touched the ground. In that moment, both of my feet were off the ground and I had no sense of where I was in space! He maintained complete control of my body by holding on to my lapel during my descent and kept my head from making contact with the mat when I landed. This is a perfect example of the power of high level of judo and its potential benefits to a law enforcement officer.

> **"The art and science of control that leads to submission."**
>
> — John Danaher

While officers can't really go wrong with any of these arts, Brazilian jiu-jitsu would be my number one recommendation due to the unique strategy when compared with the others. Ironically, Brazilian jiu-jitsu was developed based on the same critique of judo in terms of the use of strength over efficiency.

The Gracie family developed this art around applying the most efficient use of leverage to the judo techniques to allow a smaller person to defeat, or at minimum, survive against a larger opponent (Gracie, 2006). The major difference between the two arts is that judo focuses more on throwing an opponent to the ground while Brazilian jiu-jitsu focuses on the controls, sweeps, and submissions after the fight ends up on the ground. This is not to say that judo doesn't have ground techniques or that jiu-jitsu doesn't have takedowns. It's more about the points of emphasis due to the evolution of the arts. The Gracie family enhanced the ground techniques, particularly those that allow you to defend yourself while on your back. This was out of necessity due to the small size of its practitioners, namely the co-founder, Helio Gracie. This was only natural considering the fact that the smaller person is likely to end up on their back when fighting a larger opponent.

The unique contribution that Brazilian jiu-jitsu offers the police community is its concrete positional strategy based on decades of research from engaging in street fights and challenges from other martial artists. The central premise is to gain complete control over your opponent via a dominant position before attempting to submit them (Gracie & Danaher, 2003). The position over submission philosophy is also more effective on the ground due to the opponent's limited mobility and reduced ability to use the explosive energy available when standing. While a judo practitioner generally holds superior technical knowledge in taking the opponent down, the depth of understanding in escaping positions, controlling positions, and finishing an opponent on the ground is generally where Brazilian jiu-jitsu holds an advantage.

Brazilian jiu-jitsu does, however, have a disadvantage in that many of the techniques take considerable time to master. The positions often involve numerous steps and details that, when executed improperly, can lead to technical failure or being countered. These skills take many hours of repetition and sparring to hardwire the details necessary for success. The time spent honing these skills is worth it because the positional strategy of Brazilian jiu-jitsu is strikingly similar to the process necessary for effectively arresting a suspect. Officers take resisting suspects to the ground to limit mobility (i.e., keep them from running away) and control them long enough to apply handcuffs while using the minimal force necessary. This similarity makes the regular practice of Brazilian jiu-jitsu, or really any of the grappling-based arts discussed, an ideal training tool for police.

The Fourth Category

While the grappling category is most important for the needs of law enforcement, the truth is you should use it as a foundation but still explore further. Don't feel the need to limit yourself to one category. In some cases, this mindset can be dangerous. For example, if you choose wrestling as your base, maybe due to previous high school experience, you have to remember that wrestling is a sport. Wrestling does not involve strikes or weapons, but police encounters certainly do. This is where the fourth category of blending systems come into play. Whether in a formal setting or not, make sure you are getting exposure to dealing with strikes, weapons, and weapon retention. The same for if you decide to go the route of choosing an art in the striking category. Be sure that you are familiarizing yourself with ground defense and weapons defense.

Ultimately, the choice in what martial art to pursue comes down to personal preference. My recommendation would be a grappling-based art that incorporates both striking and weapons, such as practicing drills that involve defending strikes from the bottom position on the ground or fighting for a training knife that is introduced in the middle of a grappling round. That being said, the best art is really the one that you enjoy enough to pursue long term. Now that you have an idea of what arts are best for a career in law enforcement, you need to discern the qualities of a good martial arts academy.

4

Five Qualities of the Ideal Martial Arts Academy for Cops

While it would be nice for all police departments around the country to have equal access to consistent training, this is just not the world we live in. Many officers, if motivated enough to even seek additional training, have to find places on their own. This is not easy if they are unsure what to look for in a martial arts academy and already have negative perceptions of martial arts. For example, just about everyone knows someone whose child trains in martial arts. In fact, this child you know may even be a "black belt" despite not even making it to high school yet. This trend has led many to either devalue the perceived effectiveness of some martial arts or have unrealistic expectations of the skills obtained from the training. Both are mistakes. Martial arts academies are not created equal. Rather than relying on perceptions of a particular art, those who are interested should try out various academies in their area to find the right fit. In order to help with this assessment, here are five qualities to look for in a martial arts academy as a law enforcement officer.

A Good Instructor

As with starting to train at any martial arts studio, one must evaluate the legitimacy of the curriculum and instructor. For instance, martial arts academies may advertise training or techniques specifically for police officers when they have no experience, qualifications, or perspective from which to teach officers. Instructors who have not legitimately studied the law enforcement field, or been in the field themselves, should teach their art as is and allow the officers to explore its applicability to the field. This is better than attempting to speak as an expert on matters which they don't truly understand. Providing thoughts on techniques that may help officers is fine, but instructors should be transparent about their expertise, or lack thereof, in this area. There are some great martial arts "salesmen" that may have a successful business but poor-quality training, especially in understanding the unique needs of a police officer. Even good instructors can mistakenly build poor training habits or give bad advice to officers. This can often be due to lack of perspective because they've never done the job themselves. This is not to say that civilian martial arts instructors are ill-equipped to train police. That is far from the truth as there are many great civilian instructors who have made significant contributions to police training over the years. The difference between a good instructor and a bad one is the ability to adapt their martial art to the students they teach. This doesn't just apply to police officers. For example, the throws that a judo instructor chooses to teach in a class may differ if the room is full of lightweight students in comparison to heavyweight students. Certain techniques just work more naturally for a particular body type. Some techniques require adaptations to be more effective for specific individuals. An instructor's ability to pick up on this and train students accordingly is a sign that you are in the right place.

Good instructors are not bound by their martial art. They have an open mind. They ask and answer questions of their students to develop better training methods for them. If an officer has an idea that may make a technique work better for them, and it is effective, a good instructor will approve of it. They might even choose to teach it that way. If an officer has a genuine question about how a technique might apply to a real use of force situation, this shouldn't offend the instructor. It should spark interest and curiosity. If they don't know the answer, they should seek it through research and exploration and come back with an answer. These are extremely important traits. As a police officer, you do not want to be at a martial arts academy that is so stuck in tradition they are willing to sacrifice effectiveness due to a closed mind or ego. Especially when you may need the techniques you are practicing to save your life one day.

Flexible Training Schedule

The training schedule is another major attribute to consider. The work hours of a police officer can be tremendously long, variable, and unusual. It helps to have a martial arts school that offers early morning, midday, and late evening classes. I've worked day shift, evening shift, and overnight during my time as a patrol officer. Throughout each of those periods in my career, I was fortunate to train at an academy that offered classes 7 days a week including times starting as early as 5am. This variability allowed me to get my training in before or after work and still have the flexibility to train my own students as well. Even if an academy seems like the perfect place to train, not having variety in class days and times can make a difference in whether or not an officer is able to train there.

If there are no martial arts academies that offer flexible training times, consider private lessons. While they can be expensive, they often offer the individualized attention to focus on your unique needs. Splitting the fee with another officer or training partner can offset the costs. This way, even if you can only afford two private lessons per month, you can spend the time between sessions practicing the skills learned with your training partner.

Physical Conditioning During Training Sessions

Developing physical fitness is a critical component of a police officer's use of force training. Fitness can be categorized as health-related and skill-related. Health-related fitness components are muscular strength, muscular endurance, cardiorespiratory endurance, flexibility, and body composition. Skill-related fitness components are agility, balance, coordination, speed, power, and reaction time (Caspersen et al., 1985). Enhancing both of these categories and its components produce major benefits to an officer in a use of force encounter. Imagine being a county deputy on a DUI traffic stop and having to tussle with an actively resisting 250-pound intoxicated male for several minutes while waiting on backup. Imagine trying to chase down a fleeing suspect through several backyards in a residential area then having to control and subdue them when you do. These interactions would require multiple components from both categories of fitness.

This fitness training may manifest itself in a variety of ways. I am not implying your martial arts academy has to have a full gym packed with weight training equipment and treadmills. In fact, you can enhance all of the above components of fitness without any equipment. All martial arts can be taught in a way that builds these components, especially those that are more naturally applicable to law enforcement (see Chapter 3). This can be done directly through the practice of the techniques in the art or through deliberate physical conditioning being incorporated into the class. When trying out a martial arts academy, make sure you are being challenged both physically and through technical development during the training sessions.

Practical Training

> "Be careful what you practice, you may get really good at the wrong thing!"
>
> — Tony Blauer

The fourth attribute to look for in a martial arts academy is practical training. Martial arts schools vary greatly in terms of physical training methods. Some academies focus completely on the sportive aspects of the art, some stick with technical proficiency, and others are solely focused on reality-based self-defense.

You would think my recommendation would be to go straight to the reality-based self-defense school but in reality (no pun intended), that's not always the case. Each of these methods have their own strengths and weaknesses.

A martial arts academy that focuses on sport can be beneficial for police use of force encounters. Combat sports like boxing or wrestling offer consistent training against an actively resisting partner. In boxing and kickboxing, you are trying to strike someone who has no intention of allowing it to happen and has every intention of hitting you back. In wrestling, your partner is doing everything they can to prevent you from taking them to the ground and controlling them while trying to do the same to you. This type of training is not only necessary but arguably the most beneficial when it comes to preparing you for a real encounter. The two major weaknesses of the sport-focused training methods are higher risks of injury and the possibility of getting so wrapped up in the rules/standards of the sport you forget that real encounters don't have them. For example, while the tools developed in boxing will prepare you for a fight, it may be easy to forget that you can get taken down, kicked, stabbed, or even suffer a broken hand without the protection of wraps and 16 oz gloves.

Schools that focus on technical proficiency produce students with smooth, effortless movement through the execution of techniques. Performing countless repetitions build reflexive actions when the opportunity arises to execute a particular technique. As previously discussed, the enhancement of muscle memory is one of the greatest benefits of regular martial arts training. However, focusing on technique without concern for combative application under resistance lacks realism. Fights are chaotic, unchoreographed, and ugly. Practicing only with a compliant partner may build great form but it can also create a false sense of security. The raw energy and aggression of a real attacker must be experienced in training to lessen the impact of the shock factor in a real encounter. In fact, studies on police officers have found that officers performed worse under the high anxiety use of force scenarios, which simulated more realistic attacks, in comparison to low anxiety scenarios (Renden et al., 2015). Officers with additional martial arts experience performed better than non-trained officers in these scenarios. Technique training under no resistance is important for learning the proper execution of the movements, but, at some point, a sense of aliveness must be added to maximize training effectiveness.

Reality-based self-defense academies do a great job at bringing out the true aggressiveness associated with raw violence. They are characterized by their emphasis on scenario-based training under realistic situations and environments. They do not typically compete in tournaments or train under any particular sport rulesets. They address all areas of conflict, including actions that initiate conflict, the various types of combat (e.g., striking, grappling, weapons, multiple attackers, etc.), and the aftermath of an encounter. There is no doubt that reality-based self-defense academies are the best at developing the mindset of what self-defense situations are really like. This mindset is reinforced through training that is often done inside cars, on concrete, while wearing street clothes, and under adverse weather conditions.

Just as in the other academies, reality-based schools also have some weaknesses. First, a high level of aggression is often encouraged regardless of the initial attack. For instance, a reality-based self-defense response to a haymaker strike may be to block as you strike the neck with your forearm, then grab the attacker and execute knee strikes to the groin multiple times until they fall to the ground, stomp them as they attempt to get up, and run away. However, the levels of acceptable force in response to a non-lethal physical attack are not the same for civilians and law enforcement. This response may be justifiable for the average civilian, but the optics would be horrible if the exact same technique were executed by an officer. It would likely violate several policies for many departments around the country and be considered ethically and professionally inappropriate. Training at any academy where the sole objective is teaching aggressive responses to any conflict may condition an officer to react in a similar manner during encounters that don't warrant this level of force. It may be worth inquiring about options or adaptations made for law enforcement if you choose to explore these types of academies. An adaptation that all reality-based academies should implement, for example, is scenarios for law enforcement that are based on documented police encounters.

Second, while they train with "resisting" attackers, this is still usually done under scenario format. The attackers are often trained to yield to the defender's aggression rather than actively fighting back throughout the scenario. Many schools even criticize sport martial arts sparring as unrealistic and prefer this type of scenario training as an alternative. While sparring certainly has its weaknesses, the benefit is in the attribute development. Consistent sparring/live grappling under the standards of a sport, like wrestling, better develops the attribute of responding to aggression than a scenario-based attack where the attacker stops after the first act of aggression.

The above descriptions of sport-based, technique-based, and reality-based academies were not meant to imply that any particular school always trains that way. It's just something to look out for when exploring options for practical training. With that, finding an academy that has a good balance in leveraging the strengths in all of these areas would be most ideal. Regardless, practical training should be at the foundation of each session if the objective is to improve overall use of force performance.

Safe Training Environment

The fifth attribute is short and sweet but so important: safety in training. Be very careful about where you choose to train and, more importantly, who you train with. As previously mentioned, the downside to training in an environment that offers regular sparring/live grappling is the risk of injury. Whenever two people are legitimately trying to overcome one another regardless of the rules of engagement, there is a risk of injury. This is the closest you can get to the aggression associated with a real encounter on the regular basis. When training properly, the risk of injury is not much different from the risks associated with any contact sport. Injuries become more of a concern when you have bad ego-driven training partners. As a matter of fact, the more experienced your training partner, the less likely they are to hurt you in training.

To find the right training environment for you, observe a class or two when you are considering a martial arts academy rather than going straight into participating. Watch how the instructor runs the class. Do they observe and correct mistakes made by students or are they sitting against the wall on their phone while students are drilling? Check out the facility and its hygiene policies. Are the mats clean? What measures do they have in place to reduce risk of infections or sicknesses being spread throughout the gym? Check out the other students who are training. During sparring, do they use control or is everyone going as hard as they can trying to "win"? Are the beginners partnered with a more experienced practitioner to help them address any struggles they are having? Are potentially dangerous actions attempted by students addressed directly or ignored? These are just a few questions to note when considering the safe training practices of the academy you are looking into. Trust your gut when you are checking out academies for training. If something doesn't feel right, it probably isn't.

5

Five Techniques Every Officer Should Know

As discussed in chapter 3, among the various systems and categories of martial arts, grappling is the most critical for police officers. Arts like Brazilian jiu-jitsu, judo, and wrestling offer officers the most important attribute for effecting an arrest, which is subject control without the need for weapons or strikes. Developing this skill will undoubtedly improve your confidence in these situations and reduce the risk of injury to both yourself and the subject, which also leads to less lawsuits for the agency.

If you want the skill but aren't interested in committing the time to formally learning an entire system of martial arts, these are the top five Brazilian jiu-jitsu positions and techniques that are most applicable to police officers. These five movements were chosen based on a survey conducted on over 300 police officers who actively train in Brazilian jiu-jitsu (Butler, 2022). However, the positions and techniques explained below are also found in other grappling arts such as judo and catch wrestling. If you are on the fence about formal training, at least find a qualified instructor, take a few private lessons on these movements, and practice them regularly so you are prepared when an encounter goes to the ground.

> "To manage fear you only need to believe you can do things. To manage danger you must be able to do things."
>
> — Rory Miller

SIDE CONTROL

Side control offers excellent control over a subject on the ground while providing unmatched stability for the officer. There are several variations of side control in terms of the position of your limbs in relation to the subject's body. The variations pictured in Figures 1-3 are the ideal basic positions for police officers to learn. If your goal is to control the subject while applying maximal pressure, remain on your toes

FIGURE 1

while keeping your knees off the ground driving your weight into them (Figure 1). If your goal is to simply maintain control using a good stable base, keep your knees spread wide on the ground with one against the hip and the other at the shoulder. Also, use the knee (near the upper body) and arms as wedges to control the position of their head, shoulders, and elbows (Figure 2). Considering you can't always choose when

FIGURE 2

or how you land in side control, being conscious of a subject's hands in proximity to your duty firearm is critical. If you end up with your firearm side within reach, another great option is to bring your knee over the top of their forearm and staple it to the ground using the shin (Figure 3).

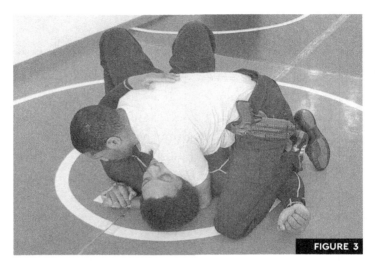

FIGURE 3

There are two core principles for maintaining this position regardless of which variation of side control you choose. The first principle is to maintain chest to chest connection, hip to hip connection, or both. This makes it incredibly difficult for the subject to move in order to get back to their feet. The second principle is dynamic movement with a constant awareness of your base. When you first put an untrained subject in side control, they will explosively push, pull, and move in various directions to try to get back on their feet. These explosive movements may compromise your base, which can cause you to lose the position or even end up on your back. When necessary, adapt your position in response to the subject's attempts to escape. This could come in the form of placing your hand out on the ground to avoid being rolled in that direction or even completely changing your position to a different variation of side control.

Police officers need to be aware of a few unique considerations when using side control. First, be conscious of a subject's attempts to access the tools on your belt. Due to the close connection required for this position, it is ideal if you have a backup unit to assist. If backup is available, they can help by controlling the subject's legs while you control the upper body. If you use side control without backup in a heavily populated area, be extra aware of your surroundings because this position can be difficult to disengage from quickly if needed. Ironically, this position can be beneficial to officers who are alone with a subject in rural areas where backup is not readily available. Holding someone in this position with adequate pressure can allow you to conserve your energy and drain the subject of their energy and will to fight, all while causing little to no physical harm. If you can build the confidence and skill to control a subject from side control, you'll find this to be a tool that can save your life on that DUI arrest at 2am when backup is 15 miles away and the subject is actively resisting arrest. Officers who don't have the luxury of a readily available backup unit must learn to slow the fight down. Rushing to get a subject onto their stomach to put them in handcuffs will likely lead to them getting to their knees and eventually back on their feet. Side control is the perfect position for patiently controlling and wearing out a subject on the ground to the point of voluntary compliance or until backup is available.

KNEE ON BELLY

"Knee on belly" is a great alternative to side control that offers less stability but better opportunities to transition or disengage quickly when necessary. It also offers a platform from which to deliver strikes. There are many methods of controlling with knee on belly. In this position, place your shin across the subject's abdomen with your toes off the ground and shoelaces braced against their hip. Plant your other leg out on the ground in line with their shoulder. Your hands should be monitoring their wrists (Figure 4) or controlling the elbows to prevent attempts to strike, grab your groin, or reach for your weapons (Figure 4b). Considering the dynamic nature of the position, you should expect to be consistently repositioning your planted foot and your hands based on the way a subject moves to escape. If you are controlling a smaller suspect and would like to reduce the pressure applied, place the ball of your foot on the ground while keeping the shin on the abdomen. If you want to increase the pressure immensely, angle your knee toward the center of their chest and drive it downward while lifting your foot off the ground.

This position can be difficult to maintain without sufficient practice. Each of these techniques discussed

FIGURE 4

FIGURE 4b

require you to devote many hours of positional sparring drills. This would involve starting in the position and working to maintain control and balance as your partner tries to escape. The position also works well as a transition from side control. For example, if you start in side control and your partner pushes against your chest in an effort to "bench press" you off of them, you can move with this energy and transition into knee on belly. Conversely, if you are controlling from knee on belly and struggling to maintain the position, you can always drop back down into side control as it is more stable. While getting good at knee on belly will be difficult to do in the beginning, it is well worth the time investment long-term.

MOUNT

The mount position is another a great way to control a subject using superior base and stability. It also happens to be a natural progression from knee on belly. Just as with the other positions and techniques, there are many variations of the mount. In this position, if your aim is maximal immobilization of the subject, keep your chest low and drive your hips into their lower abdomen. Plant your hands out wide on the ground for base and stability (Figure 5). Your knees should barely be in contact with the ground if you are effectively transitioning your weight into their abdomen. Your feet can either be in a prayer position (Figure 6) or crossed under their butt.

FIGURE 5

FIGURE 6

Placing your hands out on the ground may raise concerns if you think a subject will try to grab your firearm. To address this immediately, you can control their head with one arm and place your forearm behind the point of their elbow (Figure 7). This position will provide the leverage to slowly move the subject's arm toward their head away from the firearm. Be sure to keep the subject's head off the ground and out of alignment by lifting with your forearm and applying shoulder pressure along the jawline. Keep your hip and leg hook on your firearm side heavy and strong. This will make it extremely difficult for the subject to roll you over toward the side where you are controlling the head. Note that you can also move both elbows of the subject toward their head and clasp your hands above their head to control both limbs together (Figure 7b).

The beauty of all these positions is that you can control the amount of pressure applied. If you are mounted on top of a smaller subject, you can place more weight onto your knees to alleviate some of the pressure. You can also reapply pressure when necessary. Keep in mind that similar to the side control position, the mount can be difficult to disengage from quickly due to the closeness of the position.

Like the side control and knee on belly transitions, the mount offers a third option. From knee on belly, rather than dropping into side control as previously discussed, you can also choose to transition into mount. The same concept applies from side control in that you could move directly to mount rather than

FIGURE 7

FIGURE 7b

transitioning to knee on belly first. After becoming comfortable with each position, practicing the various transitions between them will help you learn how to maximize control over an actively resisting subject. An entire book can be written on the principles, controls, and tactics associated with these positions. This section provided a practical foundation that can be a game changer during an encounter.

MOUNT ESCAPE

The last two positions that emerged in the top 5 recommendations from the officers were actual techniques rather than control positions. The first was mount escapes. Again, there are multiple ways to escape the mount but the one pictured in Figures 8-11 is especially important because it addresses punch defense and allows the officer to reverse the position. Being stuck in bottom positions without adequate training has caused some officers to use deadly force in order to escape. Others have been knocked unconscious or even had their duty weapons taken from them.

If a subject is mounted on top of you preparing to strike, immediately control the triceps of their striking arm to defend the punch and pull down on the arm that is controlling your head while also making your head heavy to keep their arm in place (Figure 8). Trap the ankle of the subject on the same side as the arm that is holding your head (Figure 9).

FIGURE 8

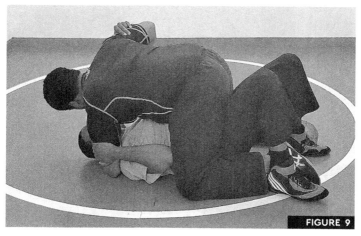

FIGURE 9

Now that you have effectively protected your face and immobilized one side of the subject's body, lift your hips up at a 45-degree angle in the direction of their trapped arm and foot (Figure 10). Considering they have no base from which to keep from falling, continuing this motion of your hips will allow you to

FIGURE 10

FIGURE 11

reverse the position and land on top (Figure 11). Be sure to continue controlling both arms of the subject and keep your head down once you land on your knees to minimize any risks of striking attempts.

The key principle in escaping a dominant position is proper timing and patience. The more energy you expend attempting to escape with no real strategy, the faster you will exhaust yourself. It is common for untrained individuals to panic in these situations and instinctively rely on strength to attempt an escape. Instead, focus on controlling your breathing and using proper technique to perform the escape. The escapes in Brazilian jiu-jitsu were designed for smaller individuals to survive against larger, stronger opponents using principles grounded in biomechanics. Consistent practice in inferior positions will teach you to trust in these techniques and effectively execute them when needed.

KIMURA LOCK

The "Kimura," which is a bent arm lock, is the fifth Brazilian jiu-jitsu technique recommended for law enforcement. This technique can be performed from nearly any position both defensively and offensively. This includes the side control, knee on belly, and mount positions discussed in this chapter. It is known as a double wrist lock in catch wrestling and a "gyaku ude garami" in judo, which loosely translates to "reverse arm entanglement." In Brazilian jiu-jitsu, the technique is referred to as Kimura in a show of respect to a legendary judo practitioner named Masahiko Kimura, who defeated the co-founder of Brazilian jiu-jitsu using the technique (Avellan, 2020).

Figures 12-15 demonstrate the application of the Kimura as a tool for weapon retention if an officer ends up on their back and a subject grabs their gun.

The instant the subject grabs your gun, immediately grab their wrist and apply downward pressure to keep your gun in the holster (Figure 12). Then, place your opposite foot on the ground, come up on your elbow as you scoot your hip back slightly, wrap your free arm around their triceps, and grab your own wrist creating a figure-four lock around the arm (Figure 13). Be sure to apply pressure into their body with your legs when you open them to prevent the subject from easily stepping over them and moving to side control. Once you have the figure four lock in place, fall back as you glue their arm to your chest, and keep your same side leg in contact with their back to minimize their chances of rolling out of the position (Figure 14). At this point, it would be extremely difficult for them to maintain a hold on the firearm. Now, apply pressure into their back with your top

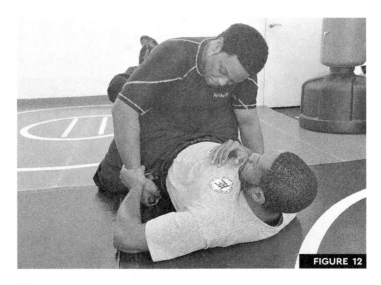

FIGURE 12

leg to free your hips and turn your shoulders to face the subject. Cross your ankles around their body and extend your legs as you rotate your upper body while pushing their wrist toward their head (Figure 15).

Remember, the power of this technique comes from the rotation of your entire body, not just

FIGURE 13

FIGURE 14

FIGURE 15

your arms. The control afforded from this position will allow you to either cause severe damage to the shoulder and elbow joint or apply enough pressure to generate compliance. At that point, you can maintain the lock, give commands for them to get off your leg and onto their stomach, then move into a handcuffing position.

Overview

These five positions and techniques serve as an excellent foundation for an officer's ground control tactics. Side control, knee on belly, and mount will help you maintain control over a subject without the need for striking. The Kimura lock additionally offers the perfect transition to handcuffing from these positions. The mount escape offers the solution to one of the most dangerous positions that an officer could find themselves in. This book is only a means to guide you in the right direction. You'll need to practice the techniques frequently to truly understand and become proficient. You'll also need to know the top five training habits to maximize your use of force training efficiency and performance while on the mats.

Five Training Habits That Will Transform Your Control Tactics

Now you have the tools to find a "LEO-friendly" training location, the martial arts options most ideal for police, and a few quality techniques to work on that were recommended by police officers. Now, let's dive into five training strategies to help make the most out of each session, even if you find yourself at an academy that doesn't focus on the unique needs of police officers. I cannot emphasize how critical this chapter is to an officer's training efficiency, especially when managing crazy work hours, family time, avoiding sleep deprivation, and still trying to find time for yourself, which is a common lifestyle for officers. When you do commit some time to training each week, you want to make it count. This first training strategy is key to doing just that.

Train with Intent

Have you ever done a training session, doesn't matter the activity, where you came out of it wondering if you actually accomplished anything? This is common in martial arts and control tactics training because we often practice without much conscious thought beyond repeating the techniques demonstrated by the instructor. Don't fall into this trap. Be present physically and mentally during your training sessions. This can be done by having a specific goal behind each training session.

Goal setting will help you build consistent effective training productivity. It is a tremendously powerful tool if you implement it correctly. Try setting short-term process and performance goals to aid in achieving your long-term outcome goals. For the sake of clarity, let's define these three types of goals (Weinberg & Gould, 2019). A process goal focuses on the specific actions necessary for optimal performance. Individuals have complete control over their process goals and they can determine what needs to be done consistently to achieve long-term success. A performance goal is based on achieving a personal standard independent of others. Process and performance goals are often a preferred focus because you have more control over the outcome.

An outcome goal focuses on the end-result, which is dependent on various factors that may be outside of your control (Weinberg & Gould, 2019). Process goals can generally lead to achieving performance goals, which will help accomplish the outcome goal. Let's apply this to an example that would serve as the perfect starting point if you are a police officer pursuing martial arts training.

POLICE OFFICER CONTROL TACTICS TRAINING GOALS

- ✅ Outcome Goal
  - ▶ During my next non-lethal use of force encounter, my goal is to effectively control and subdue the subject with no injuries to them or myself.

- ✅ Performance Goal
  - ▶ By the end of the month, I will be able to complete six 5-minute rounds of live grappling/rolling without taking breaks between rounds.

- ✅ Process Goal
  - ▶ During my training sessions this month, I will focus on controlling my breathing and using effective technique, rather than strength, to control my training partners.

As you can see in this example, the ultimate goal should be effective use of force performance, but this takes considerable time dedicated to training (i.e., process and performance goals) to achieve this outcome.

About one year into my law enforcement career, I decided to begin training in Brazilian jiu-jitsu on a regular basis. I already had some experience through my base martial arts system but one of my first use of force encounters motivated me to dive more deeply into this art. I was working a college party in the ballroom of a student center when a big fight broke out. It was about 5 minutes of pure chaos. Hundreds of people scattered throughout this near pitch-black ballroom, music blaring, and about six or seven people actively fighting near the center of the room. I ran over to the scene with several other officers and myself and another officer managed to get one of the primary aggressors on the ground. Throughout this entire encounter, my instinct was to use striking to gain control of the subject but I didn't feel this situation warranted that level of force. Once he was taken to the ground, he actively resisted our efforts to get his hands behind his back but was not aggressive toward officers. He tucked his arms tightly onto his chest and remained belly down. Three of us each controlled a separate part of his body but we struggled to free his arms to get him in handcuffs. He ignored commands to put his hands behind his back and applying pressure points did not faze him at all. I believe everyone's thought process shifted to considering other less-lethal tools, but I was eventually able to pry his arm out and apply pressure, braced with counter-pressure on his wrist and elbow to get his arm behind his back. After about 20 more seconds, we freed his other arm and applied the handcuffs.

After this encounter, I reflected on where I was prioritizing my training. Most of my life I focused on striking arts, which is not a bad choice for a young male civilian from the south side of Chicago. As a police officer, I felt it was time to shift the focus in my own training to the grappling arts as the type of encounter I just described is much more common. Shortly after this incident, I began training in the grappling arts as often as possible. In every session, I had an objective for the day. Some days, my goal was to maintain complete control over my partners on the ground, while other days it was escaping from bad positions. When we come to each training session with a concrete measurable goal for the day, we can enhance our motivation to train consistently and improve success when it really counts.

At the end of this book, there is a goal setting activity that is just like the example provided above. Think about your own outcome, performance, and process goals for your control tactics training. If you already train consistently, what are some areas of improvement that you can focus on? If you do not train on a consistent basis, use this activity as an opportunity to embark on this journey. Remember to aim for goals that are specific, measurable, action-oriented, realistic, and time-bound. You can also use the "Training Notes" pages in the back of the book to keep track of your progress and take notes on details behind the techniques you are learning in your training.

Build Your "Game" Around Punch Protection

It should be no surprise at this point that I feel a grappling-based training program is what you should pursue in your use of force training outside your agency. I would place Brazilian jiu-jitsu at the top as it relates to control tactics for police due to its versality on the ground, both while on your back or on top of a subject. However, this grappling focus should not result in neglectfully assuming that you won't get punched in the face! The techniques you use the most in training are likely to be the ones you will select under the pressure of a real encounter, so choose wisely.

In Brazilian jiu-jitsu (and many other arts), practitioners tend to build their own personal style, or series of techniques, that they frequently use in sparring and competition. This is commonly referred to as the practitioner's "game." Each individual's game is unique and often based on factors such as body size, flexibility, experience, and the influence of others (e.g., their instructor). For example, a smaller individual will likely develop a strong bottom game, meaning they will become proficient at using their legs as barriers and tools for controlling, sweeping, or submitting an opponent from their back. However, a larger framed individual may be more likely to have a top game based on takedowns, applying pressure, and control leading to a submission. Both are important skillsets to have, but with consistent training, you tend to gravitate to techniques, positions, and strategies that you naturally do well or enjoy executing.

Many grappling academies don't necessarily focus on the self-defense aspects of training. Brazilian jiu-jitsu, judo and wrestling all have strong sport influences and many programs may rarely, if ever, address how to handle being punched while grappling. This can lead to officers building a formidable grappling game based only in sport. Then, they get into a use of force encounter and reflexively obtain control positions that leave them exposed to punches. Unfortunately, this concern is often overlooked and undervalued in many sport-based grappling academies. I am not, however, implying that you should avoid any sport-based training facilities. As explained in Chapter 4, there are pros and cons to every martial arts training method. Again, the best place for you to train is the place that you enjoy enough to pursue it long term. Building the attribute of effective subject control through grappling is of utmost importance. However, if you find yourself at a sport-based jiu-jitsu academy and you notice this limitation, there is an easy fix to this problem.

You can still build YOUR game in a way that addresses punch protection. For example, one of my favorite submissions is the triangle choke from the guard position. I like this technique because it allows a smaller person to use the strongest muscles of their body, the legs, to render a larger person unconscious from their back. However, in this technique, the person has one arm free to access a weapon or punch you in the face. Years ago, I did some research on the position and learned a modification that addresses this issue. If you underhook the free arm you can both create an optimal angle for finishing the strangulation and reduce the chances of being punched. Whenever you grapple, always be aware of where your partner's hands are or be deliberate about controlling them. Please note I am not recommending the triangle choke as an ideal submission for police, although there are curricula that support it. I am simply illustrating the point that you should be thinking about these concepts when you train.

> **"Take what is useful and develop from there."**
>
> — Bruce Lee

There are thousands of techniques and positions available to build your style of grappling-based control tactics. You have to analyze what you are being taught and either make slight modifications to address the possibility of punches or don't use that particular technique as your "go to" during live training. You can and should also ask your instructor for recommendations on the best positions to explore for your game that will protect you from punches.

Build Your "Game" Around Weapon Retention

In addition to punch protection, police officers have to consider weapon retention. Whether you choose striking, weapons, or grappling arts, think about how you can build training habits that translate to the field. I'll give examples for all three of these categories. After becoming a cop, I completely changed my game in each of these ranges of combat to better fit the type of tactics I would employ on the job.

In my striking arts, I focused on sparring exclusively in a southpaw stance (which means I kept my right leg in front). I did this because I am left-handed and wanted to build the habit of keeping my weapon side back. I also spent significantly more time using techniques that I could realistically and effectively execute with a 20+ pound duty belt around my waist. In other words, my previous hook kick to the head was now a controlled oblique kick to the thigh. If you train in striking, try shadowboxing in full duty gear to see what techniques you can comfortably execute without compromising your weapons, stability, and effectiveness. These are the techniques you should focus on getting good at.

If you train primarily with weapons in an art like Kali, you learn very quickly to always expect a weapon to be present in a self-defense encounter. As a police officer, you know there are always weapons present because you brought them! For my weapons training, I focused my attention on single stick training and edged weapons defense. I emphasized single stick because as addressed in Chapter 3, the expandable baton that I carried on my belt every day was the exact same length as the rattan stick I had trained with for years. I also focused on knife defense, specifically drills that allowed me to counter the initial stages of a knife attack, create distance, and access my firearm. Many officers have the deadly misconception that immediately drawing their firearm is the appropriate response to a spontaneous knife attack. To put it simply, at close range, you have to address the oncoming knife attack first before accessing your firearm or you will get stabbed before it is unholstered.

One system that I found particularly useful for practical edged weapons training was the "Die Less Often" (DLO) curriculum within the Dog Brothers Martial Arts Association (2009). The curriculum addresses what is referred to as the "interface of gun, knife, and empty hand." It offers practical solutions for dealing with an aggressive knife attack and creating an opportunity to control the weapon or disengage and access your own weapon. These drills were pivotal in my weapons training. DLO is reality-based training done well, meaning there are scenario-based components and hard training under live resistance. Even beyond the knife training, multiple areas of combat that are not often considered, but quite critical, are trained. Examples of this include weapons access from inside a vehicle and emergency first aid for combat related injuries. The bottom line is to always train with your equipment in mind and the unique circumstances of your line of work.

My grappling-based weapon-informed modifications began with my clinch work. I started to regularly think about whether my training partners could easily access my waistline while grip-fighting in the gi (uniform) or working in the clinch. In these situations, it does not matter if they actually are attempting to reach toward your weapon side, you should still train with this idea in mind. I also worked on entering into the clinch and disengaging at will. This is simply a matter of putting 5 minutes on a clock, grabbing a training partner, and working for superior positioning in the clinch at about 50% resistance. Becoming proficient in clinch positions will allow you take the fight to the ground more easily or disengage to either protect your weapons, access your weapons, or address multiple subjects.

When drilling or live grappling on the ground, I would always be thinking about keeping my weapon side protected. This philosophy shaped both my guard from the bottom position and my top game. I developed a preference for the closed guard when on bottom, gaining control of the arm that is near my weapon side, and control of the head to keep my partner from posturing up. This limited their ability to hit me in the face or access my firearm side. From there, I focused on using select attacking sequences from this position that would still protect my face, my weapon side, and sweep or submit my opponent. From the top position, I developed a preference for controlling the hands by way of "stapling" them with my leg in side control, or bringing them above their hand when in mount, as addressed in Chapter 5. I also focused on submissions that allowed me to remain in the top position. If you train with this mindset, regardless of the type of grappling academy you end up in (sport, self-defense, or reality-based), you can build the proper habits that are applicable to your needs as an officer. That being said, it would be wise to choose a training facility that has alignment in values with your needs as a police officer. However, we are often limited to the resources available in our environment, particularly as it relates to training in person.

Build Your "Game" Around Your Department Use of Force Policy

An officer's department use of force policy often informs what options they have available to them in a use of force encounter. It's important that you understand your department use of force policy and use it to guide your training where appropriate. Taking this proactive step can help to reduce any hesitation that you may have in the field due to concerns about whether the technique you execute is within policy. It'll also allow you to focus on these techniques and tactics so you'll reflexively use them during a real encounter, rather than responding with techniques that may be in violation of policy.

Even if your department policy required only the use of techniques directly from an established curriculum, you can still incorporate it into your game during training outside your agency. If your department uses a control tactics system based in striking and pressure points, for example, you can spar using those striking techniques or variations of them to get used to applying them under pressure. During your live grappling, you can experiment with accessing pressure points by challenging yourself to obtain a position where you could apply these techniques if you wanted without your partner being in position to effectively stop it.

When I was a police officer, the only neck restraint that we were allowed to execute was a "Shoulder Pin Restraint," which is a variation of an arm triangle submission used in many grappling arts. This technique involves compression of the jugular veins on the side of the neck using the inside of the wrist, while trapping one of the subject's arms alongside their head (Siddle, 2017). This technique can be used either to control a subject until they comply or to render them unconscious. Considering this option was within my policy under applicable circumstances, I made a point to use it, or variations of it, during my grappling rounds at my martial arts academy. Any time I found myself in a position, whether standing, on my back, or on top, I tried it. I would only execute the technique by pinning my partner's right arm because I am left-handed and using the technique on the other side offers too much access to my firearm with their free hand. Although a certain level of caution should still be taken because their other hand is still free to access any weapons they may have or grab any weapons on the officer's non-dominant side. Again, these are the types of things you should always be thinking about as an officer. This consistent trial and error under pressure taught me more about the technique than any 2-day control tactics course ever could.

The reality is many departments won't allow these methods of training the techniques despite its effectiveness, but you are free to train however you'd like on your own time. It's imperative that you take responsibility for your training, even if you don't have departmental support. Train for yourself and your family members who want to see you make it home at the end of every shift.

Options When Regular Weekly Training is Not For You

Martial arts training is not for everyone. However, being physically and mentally prepared for the situations you will encounter as a police officer should not be ignored. Not to mention, living a sedentary lifestyle coupled with the stress of the job and a poor diet can buy you a one-way ticket to the grave. To put this into perspective, here are a few statistics on police officers:

- Police officers live an average of 15 years less than the rest of the population (National Police Support Fund, 2019).

- According to the American Heart Association, the average age of a police officer who suffers a heart attack is 49, in comparison to 67 for the rest of the population (National Police Support Fund, 2019).

- Police officers are more likely to be obese, have high blood pressure, and abnormal cholesterol (IACP, 2018).

These issues can be mitigated with one lifestyle change. Simply put, move more. You can do this through a variety of means, but martial arts training is arguably the best due to its dual benefits. Martial arts offer both the benefit of self-defense and improvements in physical fitness (i.e., cardiovascular endurance, muscular strength and endurance, and flexibility). If martial arts training is not for you, consider alternative options to remain active. A safe and effective exercise regimen that includes aerobic exercise, anaerobic exercise, strength training, and mobility training is an excellent starting point for officers (IACP, 2018). Despite what many martial artists may say, a physically larger and stronger individual is a force to be reckoned with in a fight. Relying solely on physical prowess means that you can either run out of "gas" in the fight or meet your match physically. These likely situations can be overcome if you have technique to accompany your physical fitness.

If you choose to focus on fitness training, my recommendation would be to, at minimum, commit to quarterly training in some form of defensive/control tactics. A great option for getting this training is through local martial arts or police control tactics seminars. These are often one- or two-day events that focus on a particular area of training. The main goal would be to make sure you are comfortable with escaping from bad positions (e.g., bottom of the mount or side control), getting back to your feet if you end up on the ground, and practical solutions for protecting yourself in a fight. You may even consider exploring diverse martial arts training options each time you seek out an event. For example, if you commit to four seminars per year on your own time, you may try out one on striking, edged weapons defense, takedowns, and ground grappling. It's all about continuing your use of force education, stepping out of your comfort zone to explore different options, and having fun with it. You may even end up finding something you like and continue to train in that area long term. The difficult part is finding the motivation to step out of your comfort zone and sign up. Just as in every use of force encounter you'll ever have, a major component of this is psychological. We will explore overcoming this obstacle of mental skill development, both in training and in real encounters, in the final chapter.

7

The Secret Weapon

"If you face just one opponent, and you doubt yourself, you're out-numbered."

— Dan Millman

Throughout this book so far, I've provided a practical guide for building physical competence for handling use of force encounters, especially for officers in agencies with minimal training resources. One area has not been emphasized even though it is the officer's secret weapon: confidence. Officers typically have the generic self-confidence most people think about as people with this trait are generally attracted to the law enforcement field. The specific type of confidence that will be addressed in this chapter is self-efficacy. In order to effectively apply any of the verbal or physical skills necessary to control a subject, the officer must believe in their ability to execute these tactics.

Self-efficacy can be defined as an individual's belief in their ability to produce a desired outcome in a specific situation (Bandura, 1997). It is essentially a situation-specific form of self-confidence. This is a secret weapon for police officers because self-efficacy is one of the strongest predictors of human performance. It can predict what actions people choose to take in given situations, the amount of effort they invest, and how hard they try when faced with obstacles (Bandura, 1977). Now, place these concepts in the context of a police officer in a use of force encounter. Picture these scenarios.

> Scenario 1: We're back at that department where officers receive the minimal standard annual control tactics training. A night shift officer at this department conducted a traffic stop on a young male suspected of DUI. Upon approaching the vehicle, he detects an overwhelming odor of alcohol emanating from the subject's breath as he speaks. He tactfully calls for back up; however, all units are currently on other calls. He decides to begin SFSTs (Standardized Field Sobriety Tests) on his own to expedite the process. After completing his DUI investigation, he advises the previously compliant subject that he is under arrest. The subject then becomes irate and tells the officer, "I

ain't going back to jail!" The officer replies in an aggressive tone, "Yes, you are!" and orders him to put his hands behind his back. The subject begins to panic, says "No," and starts walking backwards away from the officer. The officer then tries to draw his TASER and the subject unexpectedly rushes toward him, strikes him in the face, and causes the weapon to fall out of the officer's hand. The subject then mounts on top of the officer and continues to punch him in the face multiple times. Feeling defenseless, bloodied and nearly unconscious, the officer manages to access his firearm and fires multiple shots into the subject's abdomen killing him. The officer suffers a broken jaw, broken nose, and requires multiple facial stitches. His use of force is ruled as justifiable.

S c e n a r i o 2: Another officer at the same department decided about a year ago that she would take it upon herself to get the training she feels she needs. She found a local jiu-jitsu academy in a town nearby and has been training several days a week. While on patrol, approximately 6 months after the incident in scenario 1, she responds to a report of a possible burglary to motor vehicle in progress. Upon arrival, she makes contact with a male in his mid to late 30s standing next to a vehicle with a "slim jim" tool stuck inside a now damaged window frame. The officer announces herself and asks the subject to keep his hands visible. The subject immediately tries explaining that it was his car and he locked his keys inside. Shortly after running the license plate, the dispatcher makes contact with the real owner, who advises they do not know the subject. The officer briefly explains the situation and informs the subject he is under arrest. After the first handcuff is applied, the subject snatches away from the officer and attempts to run. The officer obtains a body lock around the subject's waist and takes him to the ground. She then transitions to side control and holds him down as he relentlessly tries to get away. The officer then feels the subject grabbing for her firearm, so she releases the subject's grip from the weapon by securing the firearm in the holster while "stapling" their arm with her shin. Approximately 30 seconds later, a back-up unit arrives and is able to help place the subject in handcuffs without injury to the subject or the officers.

The scenarios presented above were obviously best- and worst-case examples of use of force encounters. An officer with lower levels of training and self-efficacy in empty-hand use of force tends to be less resilient, more likely to give up on the use of control tactics when faced with resistance, and instead escalate to the tools on their belt under pressure. A better trained officer with higher self-efficacy may be more likely to use tactical communication, more effectively control the distance, make better decisions under stress, and persist using the minimal force necessary when faced with challenges. We'll address four major sources to increase an officer's self-efficacy from Dr. Albert Bandura's social cognitive theory.

Performance Accomplishments

Successful experiences performing a particular skill is the most effective way increase to self-efficacy (Bandura, 1997). Conversely, consistent failed experiences diminish self-efficacy. This is why regular control tactics training is so critical. Previous martial arts experience has been shown to produce a higher baseline of self-efficacy in police recruits at the start of the academy than those with no experience (Butler, 2020). Officers must experience success, challenges, and progress on the mats so when the real situation arrives, they have the confidence that they can execute the techniques under pressure. This again brings out the importance of live rolling (grappling), sparring, and scenario-based training. When officers are regularly executing law enforcement/policy-influenced techniques against live resistance week after week, applying these techniques on the job will be done with more confidence and control. While training that emphasizes live rolling in a grappling-based art is ideal, any martial arts training has the potential positively impact an officer's confidence.

In a training environment, you will experience failure. If you opt to train at a martial arts academy that regularly and safely trains under live resistance (which is recommended), get used to tapping out (i.e., getting submitted) or being on the receiving end of many rounds of sparring. This is a normal part of the learning process. Embrace it! Interpreting these pitfalls as if you are incapable of succeeding can cause a decline in self-efficacy. Measure success based on overall progress, not victories in training.

For example, if you just started training in Brazilian jiu-jitsu, in 3 rounds of rolling you may get tapped about 9 times. This can be extremely discouraging. Instead of thinking about it negatively, see if you can bring it down to 6 times the next time you roll. Then 3 times. Then see if you can survive all your rolls without tapping. It's a slow, steady growth process but if you see these improvements as victories, you may actually see an increase in your self-efficacy. This can increase your confidence in a use of force encounter if you end up under a larger subject on the ground after 6 months of training. Your escapes will come easily and efficiently because at that point, you'll have been there before dozens of times.

If that mindset isn't persuasive enough, think about it this way. If you go into a martial arts school dominating all your more experienced training partners during live training, that's probably a sign that you are in the wrong place. Instead of allowing your ego to cause you to quit after getting submitted by the jiu-jitsu purple belt that is half your size, take a moment to appreciate the power of the art and study it. Before you know it, a new student will walk through the door and you will be the one catching the submissions.

Another source for attaining mastery experiences to build self-efficacy is through actual force encounters experienced on the job. In a small series of focus groups conducted with veteran officers in central Illinois, experience-driven self-efficacy emerged as a major theme in explaining officer confidence (Butler, 2020). When discussing their level of confidence in use of force encounters, officers placed emphasis on the positive impact that their previous encounters had on their self-efficacy. These experiences can improve your survivability and resilience over time. However, multiple "easy" encounters can lead to overconfidence or, conversely, multiple negative experiences can lead to diminished confidence. Experiences with non-lethal force encounters benefit officers' self-efficacy as early as 6 months post-academy (Butler, 2020). Overall, experience under live resistance is key, whether on the mat or on the job.

Vicarious Experiences/ Modeling Behaviors

Observing and modeling the behavior of others, who are similar to oneself, and have succeeded in the task at hand can also increase self-efficacy (Bandura, 1997). Fortunately, in law enforcement, you are in an environment that will leverage this confidence building tactic to the maximum. This source of self-efficacy can manifest in the policing field in two ways.

First, you have decades of anecdotal experience from senior officers. If there is one thing most, if not all, departments have, it is veteran officers with stories from their years on the job. Have discussions with these officers, especially those you genuinely respect and admire, on their use of force experiences. Learn from the things they did well and the mistakes they made along the way. Veteran officers will voluntarily and happily share these stories regularly, sometimes when you didn't even ask. In general, cops like sharing their stories, especially with other cops. This is a good thing as it can be therapeutic for the veteran officer and a learning opportunity for the new officer. An ideal time to leverage this opportunity is during the FTO (field training officer) process. During this period, new officers are spending a lot of time with multiple veteran officers. Any down time can be used wisely by discussing and thinking through possible solutions to use of force scenarios that could and have occurred. During the same study addressed above, over 80% of police recruits reported they learned more about defensive tactics from senior officers and 95% of these recruits reported it improved their self-efficacy (Butler, 2020). Now, this was admittedly a relatively small group of officers (n = 105), all from Illinois, but it still lends insight to the power of vicarious learning through the use of senior officers as social role models.

The second way to leverage vicarious experiences really applies to all officers, and that is through reviewing bodycam and dashcam footage of force encounters. In this age of technology, a simple YouTube search will yield hundreds of video footage of police encounters for officers to review. Remember, observing others who you deem to be similar to yourself (e.g., other police officers) succeed can build your belief that you can also succeed in the activity (Bandura, 1977). With that, it is best for officers to observe video footage of encounters where the officer has success in controlling the situation. However, watching failed experiences of officers can be quite informative and eye-opening, allowing others to learn from that interaction. This is why every department should use roll call briefings, in-service trainings, or slow shifts to review, discuss, and analyze intradepartmental use of force encounters if allowed. The goal behind this wouldn't be to criticize the officer involved; it should be for everyone to grow and learn from the experiences of the officer. If your department does not currently do this, consider suggesting the idea to the shift sergeant. It's an amazing learning tool.

Social Persuasion

Similar to vicarious experiences, social persuasion and positive feedback can build self-efficacy. When someone gives you positive feedback on your attempts to complete a task, particularly complex one, you are more likely believe in your ability to accomplish it (Bandura, 1997). You want to train in an environment that fosters this kind of energy. From the instructors to your training partners, everyone should be building each other up. This breeds team cohesion and unity within the department, whereas ego and hyper-competitiveness is counter-productive and will likely lead to someone getting injured.

Social persuasion can also help officers discover and build upon techniques and positions that they are naturally good at (i.e., their game). For example, if an officer is consistently being told by others during the live training that she is really good at the Kimura, she may become more motivated to explore the position with even more depth and truly make it her specialty.

I recently started extensively training in Brazilian jiu-jitsu without the gi (uniform). After many years of training primarily in the gi, this proved to be a struggle in applying certain areas of my game. One of these areas were takedowns. For about a month and a half, I struggled with effectively executing takedowns during live rounds. Then, one particular week, I found success in obtaining a body lock around my partner's waist, hooking their leg with my leg and bringing them to the ground. After about 2-3 consecutive successful takedowns, these performance accomplishments boosted my self-efficacy within this range of combat. My instructor noted my progress, which lit a fire under me in terms of motivation. He commented that he noticed my consistent use of the takedown and complimented me on my skill in successfully executing it. Though he probably didn't think much of it, this simple positive feedback on an area I have been struggling with led to an intensive personal study on body locks. I studied numerous setups and finishes from the position, reached out to wrestlers I knew, and continued using it as my "bread and butter" takedown. I also now teach variations of the body lock in my control tactics courses for law enforcement. In a nutshell, words of encouragement from those you respect can significantly motivate you and positively impact your self-efficacy.

Physiological/Emotional States

The fourth area of self-efficacy enhancement, perceptions of physiological and emotional states, is critical for law enforcement. How one interprets physiological and emotional changes can influence their confidence in performing a particular task. If they see these changes as positive, energizing, and facilitative, individuals may experience enhanced self-efficacy and performance. Whereas if they see these changes as negative, debilitative, and experience self-doubt, they may experience decreased self-efficacy and performance (Bandura, 1977). While much of the research on this topic targets other populations, obviously police officers (especially early career officers) also regularly experience high levels of stress, anxiety, and arousal during encounters.

> "It's not a case of getting rid of the butterflies, it's a question of getting them to fly in formation."
>
> — Jack Donohue

This is why officers should consider preparing physically and mentally for the needs of the job as an athlete trains for competition. For example, pressure training allows an athlete in training to cope with the stress of competition. The more the athlete is exposed to stress that is similar to what they would really experience, the better they can learn to cope with it during the real performance (Weinberg & Gould, 2019). This same tactic can and has been applied successfully to police training. Studies on police performance in use of force scenarios have demonstrated the negative impact of high-pressure conditions on performance (Nieuwenhuys et al., 2009). However, training in this way actually improves performance in the long run when officers are trained in the physical skills that address the reality of a high-pressure use of force encounter (Renden et al., 2017).

During my control tactics courses, I often use pressure training methods from the field of sport psychology. Examples include manipulating the training environment via performer and environmental stressors (Weinberg & Gould, 2019). An example of a performer stressor would be having officers complete use of force scenarios without providing information on the type of attacks they will be faced with. Preventing opportunities to prepare an appropriate response simulates the rapidly evolving nature of a real encounter. Environmental stressors involve manipulating the training environment to simulate real life. This can be by way of auditory manipulation (i.e. loud distracting music in the training room) or visual manipulation (i.e. performing techniques while blindfolded). A good training drill that can get all officers involved is having participants perform the techniques learned during scenarios while others act as bystanders attempting to distract them. These distractions can involve recording the encounter on their phone or shouting criticisms at the officer for their actions. Being accustomed to environmental stressors will help officers remain focused when faced with these situations on the street.

Imagery, also known as mental rehearsal or visualization, can also be a powerful tool for officers in performing under the stress and anxiety associated with force encounters. Imagery involves simulating, or recreating, experiences in the mind to improve learning or prepare for performance (Colin et al., 2014). This practice, when performed properly, has shown improvements in performance within various fields including law enforcement. Colin et al. (2014), for example, conducted an imagery intervention study involving police officers' shooting performance under both high-threat and low-threat conditions. They found that instructing officers to imagine successful shot execution helped them to maintain their accuracy under high threat conditions in comparison to those who received no imagery intervention. While research on the positive impact of imagery on police performance is still growing, its potential benefits on coping with performance stress make it worth exploring. While the details are beyond the scope of this book, two key strategies to practicing imagery are positive thinking and using as many senses as possible.

For example, if you are interested in using imagery to prepare for your next non-lethal force encounter, visualize yourself succeeding in executing your tactics safely and effectively. Try to see the subject display the pre-attack cues that lead to the force encounter. If they are intoxicated, smell the odor of alcohol on their breath. Feel your body controlling the subject as they attempt their attack, and you respond appropriately. Hear the sound of other units on the radio advising they are en route. Remember to focus on positive thoughts, successful performance, and vivid details. The major benefit of imagery is it can be practiced anywhere, and the more you practice the better you will get at it. Consider adding this to your training routine. While it doesn't replace physical training, it is an excellent supplement that may improve your confidence and your performance.

When officers get into non-lethal force encounters, they should have at least somewhat of an "I've been here before…" experience. Granted, no single encounter is ever exactly the same but regular exposure to violence in a safe, controlled environment is critical.

A reality-based mindset coupled with training methods grounded in managing active resistance via combat sports like Brazilian jiu-jitsu, judo, and wrestling is paramount for the use of force needs of a modern-day police officer. If an officer has never been punched in the mouth, taken down and submitted in training, or performed all of the aforementioned acts of aggression on their training partner, they are likely in for a rude awakening when the real encounter occurs. Confidence and humility are best developed in the training room, which ironically reduces the likelihood of even needing the physical skills on the job. That is what makes it the secret weapon.

Conclusion

One day, I would love to see a society where all police agencies have weekly (at minimum) control tactics training, but the reality is that's just not the case right now. However, it is a valid long-term solution. In the meantime, I have a challenge for you.

Officers, set a short-term goal, let's say within the next 30 days, to seek out a training base in a martial arts or police control tactics program for your continued development in your use of force performance. You may want to revisit Chapters 3 and 4 to help guide you in the direction that best suits your interests. Then, when you find the program for you, revisiting Chapters 5-7 will help mold your training strategies to best prepare you for the needs of the job. Taking responsibility for your training is how you truly serve and protect the public and ensure you make it home every day. You are the future leadership in the policing field; these changes must start with you.

Instructors, use your skills and experience to recruit, welcome, and be a resource for the officers in your area. Use Chapters 3-5 to evaluate your own program and consider what modifications can be made to best serve your clients in law enforcement. Administrators, consider how the issues discussed in

Chapter 1 and the programs discussed in Chapter 2 can offer a foundation from which you can kickstart similar initiatives in your own department.

Civilians and retired officers, consider having this conversation with officers you know, buy them a copy of this book, and/or maybe even sponsor them for training opportunities if you have the resources. This is how we can ALL take action on the use of force problem as ONE community.

References

Adopt A Cop BJJ (2022). Our mission. Retrieved from https://adoptacopbjj.org/

Alpert, G. P., & Dunham, R. G. (1997). *Policing urban America*. Waveland Press.

Arvey, R., Landon, T., Nutting, S., & Maxwell, S. (1992). Development of physical ability tests for police officers: A construct validation approach. *Journal of Applied Psychology Monograph*, 77(6), 996-1009.

Avellan, D. (2020, June 13). *Ude garami – Origins of the kimura lock*. BJJ Eastern Europe. https://www.bjj-ee.com/articles/ude-garami-origins-of-the-kimura-lock/

Bandura, A. (1997). *Self-efficacy: The exercise of control*. Freeman.

Bandura, A. (1977). Self-efficacy: Toward a unifying theory of behavioral change. *Psychological Review*, 84(2), 191-215.

Bandura, A. (1986). *Social foundations of thought and action: A social-cognitive theory*. Prentice-Hall.

Blauer, T. [@tonyblauer]. (2016, October 8). Be careful what you practice, you might get really good at the wrong thing [Tweet]. Twitter. https://twitter.com/tonyblauer/status/784883695375245317?lang=en

Bleiker, C. (2021, March 9). National association of police athletic/activities leagues, inc. becomes official youth development partner of USA Judo. Retrieved from https://www.teamusa.org/USA-Judo/Features/2021/March/09/National-Association-of-PAL-Becomes-Official-Youth-Development-Partner-of-USA-Judo

Butler, J. M. (2020). A multi-method investigation of police defensive tactics training using a social cognitive framework [Unpublished doctoral dissertation]. University of Illinois at Urbana-Champaign.

Butler, J. M. (2022). *Is Brazilian jiu-jitsu the solution for effective police use of force performance? Perceptions of officers who train.* [Manuscript in preparation].

City Channel 4 – Iowa City. (2017). *Police practice defensive tactics with Iowa wrestling team* [Video]. YouTube. https://youtu.be/OLbd1dm_ZmE

Colin, L., Nieuwenhuys, A., Visser, A., & Oudejans, R. D. (2014). Positive effects of imagery on police officers' shooting performance under threat. *Applied Cognitive Psychology*, 28(1), 115-121. doi:10.1002/acp.2972

Dog Brothers Martial Arts Association (2009, February 13). *Die less often 1.* https://dogbrothers.com/die-less-often-promo/

Franco, S. (2021). Reality based self-defense. Retrieved from https://contemporaryfightingarts.com/reality-based-self-defense/

Gracie, H. (2020). *Gracie jiu-jitsu* (Rev. ed). Gracie Publications.

Gracie, R., & Danaher, J. (2003). *Mastering jujitsu*. Human Kinetics.

Haywood, K. & Getchell, N. (2020). *Lifespan Motor Development* (7th ed.). Human Kinetics.

Hough, R. (2017). *The future of defensive tactics: Several studies & discussions point the way forward for physical techniques training in DT*. Retrieved from https://www.calibrepress.com/2017/04/future-defensive-tactics/

IBIS World. (2021, January 22). *Martial arts studios in the US*. Retrieved from https://www.ibisworld.com/industry-statistics/number-of-businesses/martial-arts-studios-united-states/

International Association of Chiefs of Police [IACP]. (2018). Fitness Program Development Considerations. Retrieved from https://www.theiacp.org/sites/default/files/2018-09/Fitness%20Document.pdf

International Association of Chiefs of Police [IACP]. (2018). Policing in Small, Rural, and Tribal Communities. Retrieved from https://www.theiacp.org/sites/default/files/2018-11/IACP_PMP_SmallTribal.pdf

International Association of Chiefs of Police [IACP]. (2016). Practices in Modern Policing. Retrieved from https://www.theiacp.org/sites/default/files/2018-11/IACP_PMP_SafetyandWellness.pdf

Jones, J. (2010). *The path to knowledge in the martial arts: A black belt manual.* J.J. Karate Ltd.

Kano, J. (1986). *Kodokan judo.* Kodansha International.

Lee, B. (1975). *Tao of jeet kune do.* Ohara Publications.

Marietta Police (2021, February 8). *BJJ training data documents reduction in injuries.* Retrieved from https://www.mariettaga.gov/CivicAlerts.aspx?AID=3116&fbclid=IwAR2Fn2BiNzrZfJ9R8pbHXl0SSmANK1Yal-28gz22UpD7zdx_ExWgcYMufcms

Maryland Community Policing Institute (n.d.). *Examples: Community policing initiatives.* Retrieved from https://mdle.net/pdf/Examples_Comm_Pol_Initiatives.pdf

Millman, D. (2006). *Way of the peaceful warrior: A book that changes lives.* HJ Kramer, Inc.

National Police Support Fund. (2019). *Heart Disease and Law Enforcement.* https://nationalpolicesupportfund.com/heart-disease-and-law-enforcement-2/

Nieuwenhuys, A., Calijouw, S., Leijsen, M., Schmeits, B., & Oudejans, R. (2009). Quantifying police officers' arrest and self-defence skills: Does performance decrease under pressure? Ergonomics, 52(12), 1460–1468. doi:10.1080/00140130903287981

Renden, P., Landman, A., Savelsbergh, G., & Oudejans, R. (2015). Police arrest and self-defence skills: Performance under anxiety of officers with and without additional experience in martial arts. *Ergonomics*, 58(9), 1496–1506. doi:10.1080/00140139.2015.1013578

Renden, P., Savelsbergh, G., & Oudejans, R. (2017). Effects of reflex-based self-defence training on police performance in simulated high-pressure arrest situations. *Ergonomics*, 60(5), 669–679. doi:10.1080/0014 0139.2016.1205222

Roberg, R., Novak, K. & Cordner, G. (2009). *Police and Society* (4th ed.). Oxford University Press.

Siddle, B. (2017). *HFRG threat pattern recognition use of force instructor training manual.* Human Factor Research Group, Inc.

US Department of Justice. (2021). *Law Enforcement Officers Assaulted 2011-2020.* https://www.fbi.gov/services/cjis/ucr/leoka

Weinberg, R., & Gould, D. (2019). *Foundations of sport and exercise psychology* (7th ed.). Human Kinetics.

From The Author

I just want to thank you once again for reading *Stop Resisting: The Law Enforcement Officer's Guide to Proven Control Tactics, Less Lawsuits, and Building Community Trust Through Martial Arts*. This book was designed to be a quick, easy guide to take action on your journey of consistent training from hire to retire. I would very much appreciate it if you left an honest review on Amazon to help other officers and instructors decide if they would benefit from the book.

For information on my trainings, speaking engagements, or bulk order inquiries, please email policetraining@jeremybutlerphd.com or visit www.jeremybutlerphd.com.

You can also follow me on LinkedIn at https://www.linkedin.com/in/jeremybutlerphd/.

Jeremy Butler, Ph.D.

Acknowledgments

First, I want to give thanks to God because without Him, I wouldn't be where I am today. I also want to thank my wife, Nelicia, and my daughter, Nia. You mean the world to me, and I appreciate your patience, understanding, support, and feedback throughout the rigorous process of writing this book. I also want to thank my mother, Gwendolyn Butler-Watkins (RIP), for instilling in me the power of education. Thank you to all my friends and family for your love and support throughout my life.

This book would not have been possible without the support, mentorship, wise counsel, and inspiration from the following people: Dr. Michael Schlosser, Greg Cadichon, Terry Crutcher, Lazeric Hudson, Torriente Toliver, Dr. Janet Toliver, Dr. Jack Groppel, Christina Loyd, Jordan Blain, Omer Houston, Woodson Fuller, Dan Spychalski, Jennifer Bulinski, Rebecca Lewis, Chad Benavidez, Paul Sharp, and Matt Lindland.

I also want to thank the following groups, institutions, and organizations, who have been pivotal in my development as a leader, scholar, professor, use of force instructor, and martial artist: Beverly Pagoda Martial Arts Academy and my entire Pagoda Ryu family, University of Illinois Police Training Institute, University of Illinois Department of Kinesiology and

Community Health, Phi Rho Eta Fraternity, Inc., Illinois State University Police Department, Frequency Martial Arts and the entire RMNU Association, Judson University, and Five Points Jiu-jitsu.

About The Author

DR. JEREMY BUTLER is a public speaker, control tactics instructor, college professor and former police officer. Drawing from over 20 years of martial arts experience and 7 years of police experience, he regularly conducts trainings and speaking engagements for law enforcement in control tactics, verbal de-escalation, and mental performance training. He is a black belt in the Pagoda Ryu Martial Arts System, an apprentice instructor in the Filipino Martial Arts and Jun Fan Gung Fu, and a purple belt in Brazilian Jiu-Jitsu. He holds a Ph.D. in Kinesiology from the University of Illinois at Urbana-Champaign and is currently an Assistant Professor in the Department of Exercise and Sport Science at Judson University. He has written articles for *Police Magazine, Police Chief Magazine,* and *Campus Law Enforcement Journal.*

CONTROL TACTICS
GOAL SETTING ACTIVITY

✓ OUTCOME GOAL(S) (What is the desired end-result of your goal?)

✓ PERFORMANCE GOAL(S) (What quantifiable improvements do you want to see?)

✓ PROCESS GOAL(S) (What specific actions will you take to accomplish your goal?)

Training Notes

Training Notes

Training Notes

Printed in Great Britain
by Amazon

83637722R00078